TEARS
to *Laughter*
Embracing the Future Without Forgetting the Past

DEBRA DAVIS HINKLE
JIM LEONARD

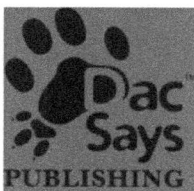

FIRST PRINT EDITION

Published by Dac Says Publishing,
San Luis Obispo, CA.

To contact publisher, email: dacsayspublishing@pacbell.net
To contact authors, email:
debradavishinkle@pacbell.net
jamesleonard08@gmail.com

www.kritiquekritics.com/tearstolaughter

Edited by Anne Schroeder and Susan Tuttle.

Text layout and formatting by Christine Taylor.
www.mousewords.net

Cover art by Sarah Danielle Campeau.

Manufactured in the United States of America.

ISBN-13: 978-0-9884076-0-2
ASIN: B006YKLF22 (Kindle edition)

DEDICATIONS

To my beloved mother, Betty Jane Davis and *to the man who didn't get away*, Roland Boothe Hinkle.
Debra Davis Hinkle

To Sophie my grandchild who died after seven months in her mother's womb, to her parents, and to her entire family.
Jim Leonard

TABLE OF CONTENTS

FOREWORD

"Grief wears too many faces," Debra Davis Hinkle tells us, and this book is a soul-satisfying soother for our hurts. Different types of loss, different stages of grief, they knock us off our center, fill our heads with sand, may cause us to question our faith, and stab our hearts at unexpected times just when we think we're doing better.

I connected with Debra in 2003 through Hospice after we both lost a parent, and learned about her unique expressive writing. For a long time I pleaded with her to come to the San Luis Obispo, CA, Barnes & Noble Children's Writing Group that I was in with Jim Leonard. After Debra joined us, our group produced *Tales From the Corner, An Anthology* and even before the anthology was published, Debra and Jim had the vision for this book. They expanded their writings and evolved this amazing book.

Debra and Jim asked me to write this foreword while I was working in Japan at a US Air Force base with military children. I started my somewhat distracted reading on a rainy Sunday, far from home and missing my recently deceased mom. I sent Debra this email, "I had forgotten the title of the book, and was in tears at times, yet also laughing, especially with your 1-800 calls to Heaven, and Best Friend and Teacher about the swearing issue, and the Finn McCool rainwater and poop quandary. I was switching from the book to emailing you, to tell you that you had brought me both to tears and the healing of laughter, when I noticed the title of the book for the first time. Wow!"

Both Debra and Jim have much to share with you in this book. We grievers have short attention spans, but this book will draw you in, whatever your loss, and speed your healing. Sometimes it just helps to know that someone else understands and has been where you are in the grief process. Debra and Jim do. "I wait for Heaven's gate to welcome me, uniting us forever more." This really is the essence of our initial loss, when all we can do is hold onto the kite string of hope of eventual reunion.

Sometimes our parents were the glue that bound our family together. We lose not only our parents, but also our siblings in the aftermath. Debra writes about the devastation that rips families apart after a loss, "We would have to forge something brand new. It can't be done when 'we' is only me." And that vise of grief that we grievers know too well, "… marbles where brain cells had filled my cerebral cavity…weighted breaths surrounded and squeezed my heart until it slowly oozed out."(**The Vise-like Grip of Grief**, Debra)

She also tells us that, "Grief isn't one-directional. It's more like an Etch A Sketch drawing—lines move up, down, side-to-side, curve and sometimes spiral out of control…" Yet she gives us a new thought, "The Etch A Sketch knobs are in your hands, From this moment on, you can draw whatever you want. Turn the knobs and start over…" (**Etch A Sketch**, Debra)

With a different type of loss, an aging parent's declining mental state, Jim offers wisdom and bitter humor. He shares, "Short-term memory loss is a bitch. There are several methods to deal with it but all of them inflict pain." He learned with his mother how good news like his granddaughter's report card cheered her and deflected emotional upsets. He writes about his difficulties in getting his mother to make plans in advance for her burial. She had rejected idea after idea until, "'I'm going to take your ashes up to your favorite casino, go up the escalator to the bingo floor, run to the back wall, and then toss your ashes all over that last row of nickel poker machines.' Following a short giggle, she replied, 'Now you've got it!' We laughed together ... like old times." (**The Perfect Place**, Jim)

Jim is a profoundly spiritual man who recognizes that grief can shake the foundations of our faith. "If you believe in me...I will see you here. Not too sure? Ask for my help...Do you not see me? Turn to the light. Hold your gaze. Focus on my face..." (**The Journey**, Jim) In missing those who were special to us, a nephew, an uncle who provided the only safe harbor, Jim's faith adds his light to bolster ours. Read **So Easily Distracted**, and be stunned by the signature.

In **Sophie's New Job**, Jim offers a unique comfort to a parent who has lost a child, a sense of reality within a dream of Grandfather-Creator calling little Sophie to share her gift of curiosity with other little ones called to Heaven. Jim teaches the healing power of laughter through the tears as he shares funny memories of a wiseacre schoolmarm with his dying mom, then to a friend to help her mom smile as the end draws near. (**Getting Velma to Laugh**, Jim)

Both Debra and Jim share how our parents live on in our memories and in who we become as adults. "I didn't know until years later that his passion had become my compulsion. Without a word, only a smile or two, his love of nature now delights my soul… It seems like I'm looking through my dad's eyes."(**Surprise Ending**, Jim) Check out **My Best Friend and Teacher** by Debra.

It can be the smell of a food our mom cooked or the perfume she wore that connects us, or as Debra says, "If you are very lucky, you feel her love and encouragement." (**Mothers Remembered**, Debra) That brought me to tears as I sat reading and writing so far from home, missing my own Haiku-poet/artist mom who had always encouraged my writer's voice since I was little.

I was grateful for the humor of Debra's memories that helped her deal with the loss of her horse, Finn McCool. "I cannot dump the water, Fill the wheelbarrow with poop, Then empty the wheelbarrow and Refill it with rainwater for the animals. It all depends on which is more important—Rainwater or poop." Read on, it gets funnier! (**The Bind**, Debra) Rarely do books touch on the profound loss of our pets that have become family. There is a heart-rending photo of her missing cat, Buff Boy, and the poignant contrast of her photo of her beloved Creampuff to her poem recounting the arrival of a box of ashes. (**The Box**, Debra) Yet, she also offers the promise that in time we can open our hearts to love again. (**Opening my Heart**, Debra)

Debra and Jim show us that whatever face of grief we are wearing, someday we can wend our way through this maze of grief and come out stronger on the other side. Whether we have lost a mother or a pet, through the slip-away of Alzheimer's or the finality of death, our memories integrate into the essence of who we are and forever-connect.

"Searching For you, For me, too, Journey begins...

Looked everywhere for you, I finally found you, In the last place, Looked inside of me, Right where you were— all the time, No longer afraid, Learning to trust myself."

(**The Last Place**, Debra)

Helen M. Sherry Ph.D. is a licensed MFCC whose passion is helping people heal from traumas and pain into happier lives. For over 30 years she has loved working with children and teens. Her books help children deal with tough issues. Helen can be reached at www.liveandgrow.com or cqhs2@me.com.

PREFACE

Debra Davis Hinkle: My inspiration for this book came from several sources. First, I wanted to repay a debt to the Hospice of San Luis Obispo County for their help after the death of my mother. Second, I thought a book might help others with their grief and healing process. Finally, I wanted the book to be an inspiration for those who want to write their own short stories or poetry.

I would like to thank my writing partner, Jim Leonard, for helping me to achieve my goals. He encouraged me and patiently read and edited my work.

Jim Leonard: My inspiration for the short stories and poems in this book came from a strong desire to help those struggling with physical, emotional or spiritual issues.

FAVORITE STORY FROM AN NBC TELEVISION SHOW

"This guy's walking down the street when he falls in a hole. The walls are so steep he can't get out. A doctor passes by, and the guy shouts up, 'Hey, you, can you help me out?' The doctor writes a prescription, throws it down in the hole and moves on. Then a priest comes along, and the guy shouts up, 'Father, I'm down in this hole. Can you help me out?' The priest writes a prayer, throws it down in the hole and moves on. Then a friend walks by. 'Hey, Joe, it's me. Can you help me out?' And the friend jumps in the hole. Our guy says, 'Are you nuts? Now we're both down here.' The friend says, 'Yeah, but I've been down here before - and I know the way out.'"

~ *Leo McGarry to Josh Lyman, 'The West Wing'*
Episode 32, 'Noel'

HEAVEN WAITS FOR YOU NO MORE

JOURNAL ENTRY: THE END JUNE 28, 2002, 7:00 A.M.

Debra Davis Hinkle, 2002

I hear a knock and stumble to the door as my sister lets herself into my mother's house.

"Debby, Mom is gone." Her words pass through me and time and space slow down like in a movie.

My mother gave me life and I don't know how to breathe, let alone live without her.

I will never be the same.

Excerpt from: Grieving Daughter, Dying Mother

"If you're going through hell, keep going."

~Winston Churchill; British Prime Minister, Historian, Writer, Artist

GRIEF IS LOSS

Debra Davis Hinkle, 2009

Loss of a loved one
Is universally recognized as grief
But it is only one kind of bereavement

Grief comes in too many faces
The empty feeling of never knowing
    a father's love
Feeling a mother's abandonment through
    alcoholism or drug addiction
Watching a parent slip away from Alzheimer's

Another face, but the same pain
If we only had a better relationship with
    our spouse or child
If only, my family hadn't fractured after
    the death of our beloved mother
If only...

A sad face, in visible pain
We bury our pets and think we can
    replace them
We cannot
They are unique, just like each of us

A wiser face, but pain never the less
We watch our fingers grasp and try to work like
    when we were young
We lose our balance and fall without ever playing
    hopscotch
Our skin wrinkles, our youth and beauty fade

Grief is loss
Loss of most anything precious and irreplaceable
Whether you feel it for six weeks or sixty years

"All things bright and beautiful,
All creatures great and small,
All things wise and wonderful,
The Lord God made them all."

~ *Hymn by Mrs. Cecil Alexander*

MY LITTLE ONES: SHELLY AND MORRIS

Jim Leonard, 2012

Shelly was my beautiful orange shorthair female tabby. She could run like the wind, catch mice, lizards, and birds, and then bring them inside as toys. She was bold around people and begged for belly rubs. She had very soft hair and liked to be touched to get her little motor running. On April 25th 2012, she died in the hospital of an unknown blood disorder. I miss her terribly.

She loved playing with her toys. One of them looked like a bumblebee and she would toss him up over her head, jump, and catch him in mid-air, juggle him with both paws, and then roll on the floor with him. I knew she was delighted with this action. Many times, I watched her perform with the little bee and I was always amazed at her agility and immediate response to his flight position.

She was a surprise gift from my granddaughters in

October 2005 along with her brother Morris. Shelly brought me so much joy and happiness. Each night as they got into my bed I thanked the Creator for them. I know he loved them too, maybe even more than I did. My night time prayer also thanked the givers for their thoughtfulness and generosity.

In May 2012, I received a very beautiful urn with her name on it. I haven't figured out where to place the urn in my house. But I do know she will be buried with Morris and me.

Morris was my beautiful orange shorthair male tabby. He was Shelly's brother (but not from the same litter). I usually had to coax him into action because he was very shy. His favorite trick was to hide and ambush Shelly.

They would grasp each other and wrestle for a short time. Normally, he wasn't fast enough to catch her, so after most attempts he whimpered softly and then went to his food bowl. On April 27th 2012, he died in the hospital following blood and liver problems. I miss him very much, too.

Morris loved for me to pick him up and hold him on

my left shoulder. Then with my left arm under him, I would swing him out so he could see the view. With his mouth closed he looked like he was smiling, and I am quite sure he was. He also loved playing with his toys. He would wait for me to get on the floor and move each one and he would grab some and play keep-away. Shelly would join in on the action too. At night when we all were in bed, he loved to stick his nose into my beard. I loved for them to sleep with me.

When Morris first got sick, he simply stopped eating. A veterinarian told me if we could get him to eat on his own his blood and liver problems might go away. I simply did not want to lose him and I was willing to try anything that might save him. The hospital inserted a feeding tube in his throat and I fed and medicated him for about two months without success. Late in this process, I came to realize that some of my actions were causing him pain. One evening I was attempting to clean him up a little and he started to cry out because I was keeping him from rolling over. That sound of his cry pierced my heart and soul. Then I knew it was time to let him go. The next day I held him gently as the doctor put him to sleep. It was a peaceful process and I was very proud of him.

In May 2012, I also received a matching urn with his name on it. I haven't figured out where to place it, either. But I do know he will be buried with Shelly and me.

"God will prepare everything for our perfect happiness in heaven, and if it takes my dog [cat] being there, I believe he'll be there."

~ *Billy Graham; Preacher, Evangelist*

PHOTO – SHELLY AND MORRIS

The Co-Author's companions on their favorite resting place.

Photo by Jim Leonard

JOURNAL ENTRY: WEDNESDAY, MAY 29, 2002

Debra Davis Hinkle, 2002

"When will Grandma's last day be?" my ten-year-old nephew asked.

"Why, honey?"

"So we can make it a really good day for her," Kyle said.

Excerpt from: Grieving Daughter, Dying Mother

"The human heart is always drawn by love."

~ *St. Catherine of Siena; Nun, Christian Writer, Theologian, Scholar*

BUFF BOY...

Debra Davis Hinkle, 2009

Found
Fed
Tamed
Raised
And loved you so

Muscle
Speed
Strength
Stamina
Of a wild being

Handsome
Buff colored
Pale orange stripes
Tipped left ear
Of a feral cat

Favorite
Timid
Sweet
Quiet
Except for your loud purr

Five hundred, ninety days later
Disappeared
Missing
Vanished
Purr no more

Your playmate
Waits
Paces
Longs
For your return

I
Search
Pray
Cry
For you

You've fallen prey to an
Owl
Coyote
Mountain lion
Fate can be so cruel

Accepting your death
Painful
Heart breaking
Final
Must say goodbye to you

*   *   *

Heaven
Waits
For
You
No
More

I
Wait
For
Heaven's
Gates
To
Welcome
Me

Uniting
Us
Forever
More

"There are few things in life more heartwarming
than to be welcomed by a cat."

~ *Tay Hohoff*

PHOTO - BUFF BOY

Debra's Cream Colored Tabby.

Photo by Debra Davis Hinkle

In June 2007, I found a dozen feral cats and kittens in a dry creek bed behind my house. Buff Boy was one of the three month old kittens. I spent the summer and fall taming the colony. Unfortunately Buff Boy was killed before his second birthday, on January 31, 2009.

SHE AND I

Debra Davis Hinkle, 2008

We're blood
Sisters
Sharing both mother and father
Only eighteen months between us
Similar hair and eye color

More than childhood shared
But little familiarity
Even less bond

Her soft and sweet voice fills my ears
Not forgotten, although unheard for five years
Mine strong and hardly melodic
Possibly remembered

Anger that masks a well of pain
Now a state between us
I've an idea how we got here
She has her feelings, too

A monstrous void
Little hope of ever getting back
What was lost or
What was never there

I don't want to go back
When there's nothing there for me
We would have to forge something brand new
It cannot be done
When we is only me

We share so many things
Where is the usual bond?
Why don't we share our love?

What I'm really saying is—
I love her
Why doesn't she love me?

I hate the answers

"Grief is the price we pay for love."

~ Queen Elizabeth II

JOURNAL ENTRY:
TUESDAY, JUNE 25, 2002

Debra Davis Hinkle, 2002

My mother's doctor is kind and patient explaining that her kidneys have stopped working and the tumor markers are going up.

"Your mom has liver cancer now."

That information and a whole lot more took the direct tunnel route from one ear or both to the long lost non-retrieval area of my brain. A lot of things have fallen down that tunnel recently.

I wonder if there is another access to the storage area. With my luck the coding system is a series of 0's and 1's and only a computer hacker could find the back door and the password.

Excerpt from: Grieving Daughter, Dying Mother

SHE MISSES

Debra Davis Hinkle, 2008

His
eyes
that sparkle and dance

His
squeezes
hugs and kisses

His
rough hands
that caress so gently

Where is her husband?

She feels half-alive
Without her man
Is she woman?

THE LITTLE GIRL AND HER CAT

Debra Davis Hinkle, 2011

"Mommy, Tabby got hit by a car and died."

"Don't worry, we'll go to the pound and get you a new little kitty."

"But I want the old one."

"It will be okay."

"If I die, are you going to replace me, too?" asked the little girl.

"The smallest feline is a masterpiece."

~ Leonardo Da Vinci; Italian Renaissance Polymath

JOURNAL ENTRY:
FRIDAY, JUNE 28, 2002

Debra Davis Hinkle, 2002

I'm having trouble falling and staying asleep, but I'm not having nightmares. I guess my mind can't conjure up anything worse than the horror of waking up without my mom.

Excerpt from: Grieving Daughter, Dying Mother

"The weird, weird thing about devastating loss is that life actually goes on. When you're faced with a tragedy, a loss so huge that you have no idea how you can live through it, somehow, the world keeps turning, the seconds keep ticking."

~ *James Patterson: American Writer*

THE VISE-LIKE GRIP OF GRIEF

Debra Davis Hinkle, 2009

When I turned fifty
Grief over my mother's death
Smacked me in the face
Placed marbles where brain cells had
Filled my cerebral cavity
Crushed my lungs leaving me
Feeling weighted breaths
Surrounded and squeezed my heart
Until it slowly oozed out

"If you have ever lost a loved one, then you know exactly how it feels. And if you have not, then you cannot possibly imagine it."

~ *Lemony Snicket (pseudonym), Daniel Handler is an American author and screen writer.*

THE BOX

Debra Davis Hinkle, 2008

It arrived today, just nine days after we ordered it. It's small—only two and half by three by six inches. It's nice enough looking. A golden oak shade—it looks like wood, but it's not. I keep it on my desk near me. I find myself reaching for it, running my hand over the top. It's smooth to the touch, but it doesn't feel the same.

But! There's always a "but," and this one's a big one—the box doesn't PURR. It doesn't rub up against my legs. It can't sit in my lap or walk across whatever I am trying to read or write. It doesn't beg for my chocolate milk or for pieces of my turkey sandwich.

I'll never be able to run my fingers through your soft, silky fur. The early wake-up calls with your sand papery tongue are no more. Forever gone are the high-pitched meows of a blue cross-eyed flame point Siamese boy.

Creampuff, you gave me almost eighteen years and the

only thing left to give you was to be there when your heart stopped—touching you like you touched me.

"Until one has loved an animal, a part of one's soul remains unawakened."

~ *Anatole France; French Poet, Journalist, Novelist*

PHOTO – THE BOX

Creampuff's Memorial Urn.

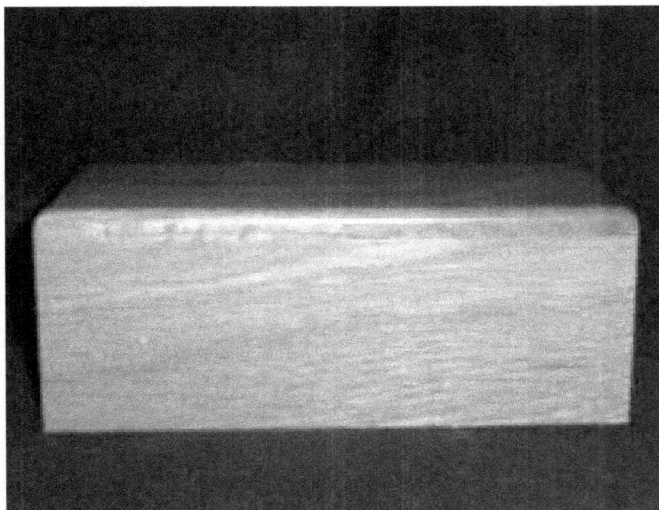

Photo by Debra Davis Hinkle

The box sits in my office near where Creampuff used to sleep. His favorite spot was on top of the computer monitor (old style), curled up in his soft and padded leopard printed cat bed. (See next photo.)

PHOTO - CREAMPUFF

Debra's very handsome Flame Point Siamese.
(In America he was classified as a Red Color Point
Shorthair.)

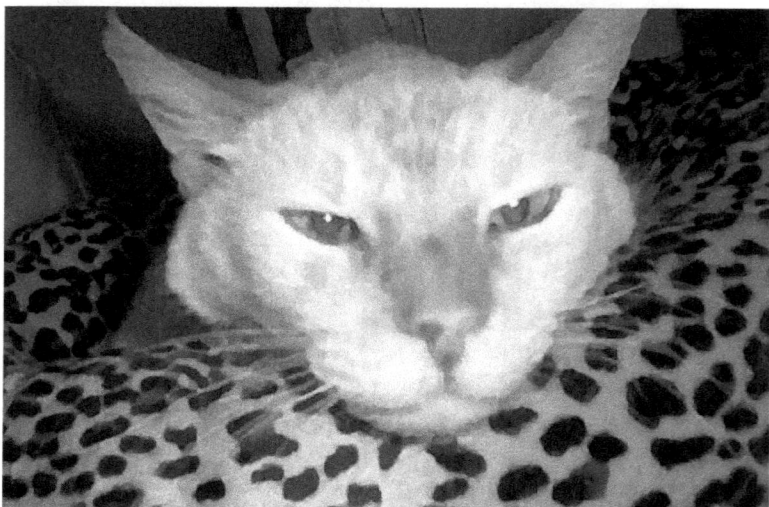

Photo by Debra Davis Hinkle
(Enhanced in Photoshop)

Creampuff was adopted in 1990 from the Los Angeles County Carson Animal Care Center. I volunteered, on Saturdays, at the shelter and saw the Flame Point Siamese kitten. When the kitten became available for adoption, the following Tuesday morning, I was waiting at the Shelter's main door. Creampuff was eighteen when he died in 2008.

PAINFUL COMMENTS

Debra Davis Hinkle, 2011

After the death of my mother, nine years ago, I was often livid with people who were trying to help me. At the time, concerned and compassionate people would say things to comfort me. But they completely missed the mark.

Here are a few of the completely inappropriate comments and my thoughts: "You will get over it." *How the hell do you know?* "She's with God now." *I wish he'd give her back.* "She's in a better place!" *What if there isn't a better place?* And my favorite, "Aren't you glad she's with Jesus?" *No, I'm not—I want my mother back.*

Nine years later and after reading *The Grief Recovery Handbook* by John W. James and Russell Friedman, I can intellectualize my grief and understand what was happening to me after her death. I know that their comments were meant to be kind, but my feelings still remain the same. I hope in the future I can skip the feelings of anger or at least have it trigger a sense of gratitude. I also hope to remember to just say, "I'm sorry" when someone else is grieving.

A friend who read this story for me said, "It has to help knowing that others cared enough to want to do the impossible — take the hurt away." Thank you, Susan Tuttle.

"I can't accept the reality that you are gone. That I won't hear your voice again ..."

~*Anonymous*

ETCH A SKETCH

Debra Davis Hinkle, 2009

Grief isn't one-directional.
It's more like an Etch A Sketch drawing—
lines move up, down, side-to-side,
curve and sometimes
spiral out of control.

When the image becomes clear,
with just a movement,
the picture distorts or disappears.
Life can be erased by a mere shake—
creations can be lost, forever.

It can never look the same.
Life will feel fleeting and unsteady,
with your foundation gone.
How can you re-build it?
Where do you start?

The Etch A Sketch knobs are in your hands.
From this moment on,
you can draw whatever you want.
Turn the knobs and start over—
that's all we can do.

JOURNAL ENTRY:
WEDNESDAY, JUNE 26, 2002

Debra Davis Hinkle, 2002

"Mom?"

"Yes, honey."

"Would you make a place in Heaven for us, like you did on earth?"

"Of course, honey."

Excerpt from: Grieving Daughter, Dying Mother

"Out of suffering have emerged the strongest souls; the most massive characters are seared with scars."

~ *Khalil Gibran; Lebanese-American Artist, Poet, Writer*

You Come, Too

Debra Davis Hinkle, 2008

I wouldn't feel alone
If we were together
For now
For always
You come, too

Inspired by Robert Frost
"The Pasture."

"I'm going out to clean the pasture spring; I'll only stop to rake the leaves away (And wait to watch the water clear; I may): I shan't be gone long, -- You come too."

~ Robert Frost; American Poet

HELPING HAND

Debra Davis Hinkle, 2009

Dedicated to Kyle Taylor Murphy

My mother's graveside service
His grandmother's
He sat with his three aunts and cousin
In the first row

In the second row
Sat his mother and father
My husband, aunt and uncle, too

He was ten
I was fifty
I should have comforted him

My sister gave me a tissue
When I began to cry
And, he held my hand

Second Place winner in the Lillian Dean Contest, 2009.
Printed in SLO The Tribune, April 12, 2010.

CONVERSATION: 2004

Debra Davis Hinkle, 2009

"When did you stop doing crossword puzzles?" my husband inquired of his ninety-one year old mother.

Mom responded, "I stopped when I lost my mind, honey."

"It is a fearful thing to love what death can touch."

~ Anonymous

THE PERFECT PLACE

Jim Leonard, 2008

Short-term memory loss is a bitch. There are several methods to deal with it but all of them inflict pain. The memory just sits there laughing at you and the harder you try the more it laughs at your feeble efforts. My mother was frustrated with the condition in her later years and our combined attempts to relieve her pain were of little use. This story relates some of our experiences.

I moved my mother into an assisted living environment in Orange, CA during October of 1998. She was 84 at the time, widowed nearly 20 years, pretty set in her ways, but realized that she needed help. I'm her oldest son. We had lived together since my father passed away in 1982. My strategy for dealing with her forgetfulness was to change the subject of the conversation, especially if we were talking on the phone.

While I was working in Fort Worth, Texas, I called her every evening. After listening to her for a few minutes I could sense her emotional state. If she was happy I would begin discussing what was happening with a family member. If she was excited, agitated, or crying I would immediately interject something to get her attention like, "Hey Mom, let me give you some good news."

"OK, tell me about it."

"I've got a copy of Carly's 2nd grade report card and it's so good, just listen to this: English, A; Math, A; Science, A." I read every line on the card to her.

Mom replied, "She's a pretty smart little girl. She must get that from me."

I said, "Her English teacher also noted, excellent in reading comprehension. You know what that is, right?"

"Yeah, it means understanding. I'm not stupid, you know."

"I know Mom, I was just checking."

After a short pause, she remarked, "Oh thanks so much, all I needed was just a little good news. Call me tomorrow."

* * *

On one of my trips to visit with her, I asked, "Do you want to go for a ride?"

"Yeah, let's get out of here."

It was mid-morning and I knew what she loved for breakfast. "Want to stop somewhere and get some coffee?"

She replied, "And a couple of doughnuts too."

Sitting at a little table near a window we reminisced about the old days.

* * *

On another trip, I was driving her around the city and she began telling me about her dream. "Last night I saw my dad standing near his gravesite."

I didn't want her to be talking about death, so I quickly remarked, "Oh, that's not important. Let's talk about something else." She became very quiet and when I looked over at her she was starting to cry. I stopped the car, moved over close and hugged her. "I'm so sorry Mom. I didn't mean to make you cry."

"I know, but it was important to me… and I wanted to tell you about it." Then she related her dream to me.

"Was your father talking to you? What did he say?"

"I don't know. I think it was something about my mother."

We didn't know what to make of it. Later, thinking about the dream, I concluded it may have been a recurring dream. One she hadn't shared with me before. I knew her mother had died giving birth to my mother.

*   *   *

I called one evening and noticed she was happy. So I took the opportunity to discuss something that was bothering me. "Mom, you know we have those two gravesites out there in the desert. But, now I don't think it's such a good spot."

She replied, "I don't either."

Hoping she would say California was okay I continued the discussion. "I was thinking about Southern California. We would be near family, close to where we sprinkled Dad's ashes in the ocean; it's a good climate, with plenty of flowers. Does that sound good?"

"No. I don't think so."

"Well how about the Central Coast of California? Also near family, nice climate, near the ocean, and lots of flowers. Just like your favorite spot in Carmel."

"No. I don't like that either. Nobody would go way up there just to visit me."

After a short pause, I continued, "OK if that's the case I know exactly what to do. I'm going to take your ashes up to your favorite casino, go up the escalator to the bingo floor, run to the back wall, and then toss your ashes all over that last row of nickel poker machines."

Following a short giggle, she replied, "Now you've got it!"

We laughed together … like old times.

* * *

In September of 2000 my mother passed away during hip replacement surgery. The doctor told me her blood pressure went way down—never came back up, and she passed away peacefully. The evening before her death, my oldest daughter was with her. They laughed about going dancing together after the operation.

I didn't follow-up on the casino plan. She rests alongside a site I prepared for my dad in the Valley of the Bears near Montaña de Oro, a California State Park. I had a few mementos he left with me. I buried them and placed the following on his gravesite marker. "He loved tinkering with Lionel Trains, helping others, exploring the Western US, and he quietly taught us to love Mother Nature." Next to him, her marker reads: - "She loved to dance, follow the rainbow, and she excitedly taught us to follow our heart while seeking the spiritual." Soon I will take my place next to her as it was destined from the beginning of the universe.

"Sometimes the heart sees what is invisible to the eye."

~ *H. Jackson Brown, Jr.; American Author, Inspirational Writer*

PHOTO – THE CO-AUTHOR'S PARENTS

Jim & Myrtle Leonard in 1933 after their marriage.

Photo is part of the Co-Author's family album.

JOURNAL ENTRY: THURSDAY, JULY 18, 2002

Debra Davis Hinkle, 2002

Alone in Mom's empty house, I said my goodbye—I thanked her for the home she made for me.

Walking out that door was one of the hardest things I have ever done.

Excerpt from: Grieving Daughter, Dying Mother

"Why does it take a minute to say 'Hello' and a lifetime to say 'Goodbye'?"

~ Anonymous

SOMEDAY HEAVEN'S GATES WILL WELCOME ME

JOURNAL ENTRY:
SUNDAY, JUNE 23, 2002

Debra Davis Hinkle, 2002

Five days before my mother's death, surrounded by her four daughters in her hospital room, a funny moment just happened.

The doctor walked into my mother's room. "Hello, Betty, how are you doing?"

My older sister asked, "Mom, do you know who he is?"

"God!"

"No, they just think they are," I piped up.

Dead silence for the next few seconds—then the doctor breaks into a heartfelt deep laugh—my sisters, collectively, exhaled and laughed, too.

We all laughed—our last laugh as a family.

Excerpt from: Grieving Daughter, Dying Mother

1-800-HEAVEN*, FIRST CALL

Debra Davis Hinkle, 2008

I don't know why I keep calling this number—it's been busy for over four years. Oh, my God, the telephone is ringing! I must have misdialed. It couldn't be ringing up in HEA—

"Hello."

"MOM, is that … is that really you?"

"Yes, honey, it's me."

"I'll be damned."

"Honey, how many times have I asked you not to swear?"

"Oh, Mom! … I miss you so much!"

"I miss you, too!"

"Why did you leave me, Mom?"

"I didn't leave you. It was just my time to go."

"I almost didn't make it without you!"

"But, you made it, and now you're happy again."

"How do you know that?"

"I just do, honey."

"Mom, just before you left you said—"

"—'DEBBY, I REALLY, REALLY LOVE YOU!'"

"Mom, that helped a lot in the dark times."

"I'm glad, honey; but it was meant to make up for a lot in the past."

"I know! Mom, may I call you again?"

"Yes, but I've got to go now."

Click!

DAMN, she hung up on me! *Oops, hope she didn't hear that!*

"If there were visits to Heaven I would be first in line if it meant I got to see you one more time. I miss you more every day."

~ *Anonymous*

CONVERSATION: 2005

Debra Davis Hinkle, 2010

"Honey, please don't let them reincarnate [resuscitate] me," my husband's ninety-two year old mother said.

"Don't worry Mom, I won't let them reincarnate you," my husband responded without acknowledging her faux pas.

"Love begins by taking care of the closest ones – the ones at home."

~ *Mother Teresa of Calcutta*

THE JOURNEY

Jim Leonard, 2008

If you believe in me
  I will see you here.
Not too sure?
  Ask for my help.
Do you want the truth?
  Listen to my words.
Are you looking within?
  Feel my fire.

Do you not see me?
  Turn to the light.
Hold your gaze.
  Focus on my face.
Is that you or me?
  Touch my hand.
Now you know…
  We are one.

THE VASE

Debra Davis Hinkle, 2009

It is not—
    cut crystal or from Tiffany's,
      an antique or expensive,
        one of a kind or even unusual.

It is—
    just a small green and gold oriental vase,
      one of thousands or tens of thousands,
        something you could get at Pick-'n-Save.

But, to me—
    it is beautiful,
      my favorite,
        more precious than a Ming vase.

My mother gave it to me.

PHOTO - THE VASE

Debra's vase.

Photo by Debra Davis Hinkle

The vase was a gift from my mother. It is mint green and gold foil in an oriental pattern. The vase is displayed in my bathroom so the shape, pattern and colors can bounce off the mirrors in all directions, reminding me of my mother.

SOPHIE'S NEW JOB

Jim Leonard, 2008

It is mid-February in Santa Ana, CA and the air is clean and clear, revealing snow covered mountains on the northern skyline. A young couple is asleep and dreaming about their soon-to-be first child. As they sleep, his hand rests on her stomach. This posture induces a recurring dream for him and he loves it.

In the dream a little girl named Sophie and her mommy and daddy are camping in the mountains. This particular early morning she is wide-eyed with excitement while prancing in a shallow stream. Her daddy watches the action and becomes fascinated at her gleeful curiosity. She calls-out, "What color is this petal? How come the bees love this flower so much?" He could hardly wait to explain these things to her.

Unknown to Sophie and her parents another observer enters the dream. Far, far away Grandfather, the

Almighty Creator of heaven and earth, is pondering their delight from his vantage point beyond the universe.

The dream continues as Sophie is exploring her newfound world. A heavy mist engulfs the trees giving their campsite a magical quality. Camping is a new experience for Sophie and it brings so much joy that she can hardly keep from shouting. Her turquoise eyes are wide open as she scampers around their campsite. She isn't tall enough to step up onto the seat of their picnic table but she manages to climb up there to wait for her daddy. Her golden hair glistens as the morning sunlight breaks through the mist.

"Daddy, please hurry, come with me to that little stream." He smiles, reaches out for her hand, and they start walking toward the stream. Her awe of nature, the treasures she finds, her enthusiastic responses produce a hypnotic effect on him. He is resting in the grass, intently staring at her playing in the stream, she fades into the scenery, and his dream takes another turn.

Grandfather smiles while keeping his attentive gaze on them.

Sophie is sitting on her bedroom rug quietly arranging toys in her playhouse. An unusually bright radiant yellow glow radiates from her. She hears someone calling her name. "Here I am. Who is calling me?"

"Sophie, I am the Creator, I am sometimes called Grandfather, and I love you very much. I created you to play with me in my beautiful garden. I know you love your parents very much, however, now it is time for you to come home with me."

The tone of his voice, seriousness of his message, and his peaceful manner helps Sophie sense that Grandfather is speaking truthfully. "Oh no, Grandfather, it is much too soon for me to leave this beautiful place. Can't I stay just a little longer? My daddy wants me to play with him today."

"I'm sorry child but you cannot stay. Your life here is ending and you are coming to live with me. Some of my little ones require your help. They need someone to help them develop a curious spirit – to seek, to ask, and to behold my creations. A curious spirit is very pleasing to me. Your curiosity is a gift from me, and it is something you can share with the children. They will love you for this gift and in turn, they will love me all the more. Teaching them to be curious is a wonderful job for you. Now go, you just have time to whisper your goodbyes."

Sophie weeps. She wants to run, play, and explore with her daddy. She muffles the sound of her sobbing, tiptoes into their bedroom, kisses them both on the cheek, and quietly whispers, "I love you both so much. And Daddy, we will do all of the things you wanted – only later in Grandfather's garden."

Grandfather and his angels gently bring Sophie home on eagle wings. She will dwell in his garden for all eternity – playing with him and his little children.

As Sophie ascends to Grandfather's home her daddy wakes from his dream. He cries out to his wife. "Sophie has been taken from us. I saw her kiss us both on the cheek, I heard her whisper that she loves us, and then angels carried her away." They reach for each other, embrace, and both begin crying, uncontrollably.

Far away, Grandfather also weeps. Sophie pleads, "Hear their cries Grandfather. Please have your angels console them." Grandfather sends them his comforting gifts of compassion and understanding.

Again, Sophie is wide-eyed with excitement, only now she is dancing with Grandfather and his little children in an extremely beautiful garden. Her eyes are brilliant turquoise as sunbeams glisten off her golden hair.

Footnote: Santa Ana, California (6/08/2005), a little girl died during childbirth after seven months in her mother's womb. She had been in their dreams for many years. This event inspired "Sophie's New Job" to comfort those grieving and their caretakers.

Sophie's sister, mother, father, and grandfather have been somewhat consoled about their loss by accepting it was God who created her and he has called her to be with him in heaven. Sophie was the author's granddaughter.

Updated story from Tales From The Corner, An Anthology,
Central Coast Press (2005)

"A little thing the size of a hazelnut … In this little thing I saw three truths. The first is that God made it; the second is that God loves it; and the third is that God sustains it."

~ *Julian of Norwich, Revelation of Divine Love,
Mystic, Theologian*

NOT ONE DAMN DAY MORE

Debra Davis Hinkle, 2008

Every day that I didn't talk to him was painful
I couldn't let four years pass

*   *   *

Departure with "I love you" in sign language
He so proudly taught to me while visiting
Then he didn't return my phone calls
Clearly, my nephew was ignoring me
Usually a child doesn't abandon an adult

Shocked and then puzzled
I wondered why
What could I have done wrong?
I searched the past
I found nothing

Still, I looked for a reason
If only, I found the cause
I could fix it
I would have my nephew back
Things would be okay again

Abandoned, again
Who was left?
Would it be only me someday?

It felt like another death
Mom died only eighteen months ago
Shock and puzzlement had turned to grief

Pain deeper than I thought possible
Frustration, too
Anger, occasionally

Later the deep pain slowly melted into a boiling anger
Anger felt better than the bleeding pain
I was abandoned, again

A thousand days passed
Before anger receded
Love once again filled its place

I couldn't let four years pass
Every day that I didn't talk to him was painful
Not one damn day more
Today was the last day, hopefully
I reached out with love and forgiveness

*   *   *

When it was time,
He reached back

UNCLE BOB'S GIFT

Debra Davis Hinkle, 2008

No one seemed to care
Or even notice the
Little, bruised and scared child

Uncle Bob did, though

He unlocked the closet door
He set me free from—
The dark and scary place
Held my hand and listened, too

*　*　*

How do I say
Thank you
To the man who loves me,
The way my father should have
But never could?

I hope you know
That when I fell out of the tree
And, you comforted me
I felt your love

I hope you know
That besides the
Toy nurse's kit
You gave me self-esteem

I know you know
When I call or visit you now
That I cherish our time together
However, short it might be
The gift of your love will endure

"… love knows not its own depth until the hour of separation."

~ *Khalil Gibran; Lebanese-American Artist, Poet, Writer*

PHOTO – DEBRA AND HER UNCLE

The photo was taken at The Loading Chute in Creston, CA in April 2011.

Photo by Roland B. Hinkle

CHANCE ENCOUNTER: 2002

Debra Davis Hinkle, 2009

During my mother's final illness and after her death, it seemed I couldn't go anywhere without breaking into tears. Once when I was in the dentist's office, I broke down while paying my bill. A woman waiting next to me just spontaneously hugged me.

It was sorely needed, at the time. Looking back, I find it amazing for two reasons. First, she reached out to a stranger in great pain. Second, her daughter was standing next to her—she showed her child something greater than anything she could have tried to tell her— the kindness she passed on to me.

"At the end of our life, we shall all be judged by charity."

~ *St. John of the Cross*

SO EASILY DISTRACTED

Jim Leonard, 2006

Over these last few weeks the situation has become unbearable. I've tried to articulate my feelings to my father and ask for his help. My latest attempt goes like this:

Dear Dad:

I miss you so much. The job you gave me seems to be taking forever. As you know, I'm close to the end of this teaching assignment. I do look forward to seeing you soon.

The little creatures down here do love me as you said. They play all kinds of tricks and antics to please me and to keep my attention on them. Now I understand why you love them so; they bring joy to my heart too.

While walking with each one, I've explained all your words. Each time I see a glimmer of understanding in their eyes; they follow up with a question that is totally off the point. It is frustrating because I know they are capable and it will be so exhilarating for them to sense you again. Many times I've shown them the path home. I personally placed each one on it, walked along for a while, and sent them on to you.

I have serious doubts regarding the success of my task. They are so curious about everything and are so easily distracted from staying focused on finding you. Any little thing that moves or happens to catch their eye sends them off in a totally different direction. And to make matters worse, getting the new thing becomes an obsession. Upon getting it they happily bring it back to me and by then they have forgotten all about finding their way back home to you.

These little busy bodies have such limited scope for imagination. When I remind them about your marvelous house, your creativity, your desire for them to be near you, their eyes glaze over resulting in a blank stare, which says they haven't got a clue; they simply do not remember.

I've managed to train a few of the elders from various

groups who are capable of teaching the others. So given a little more time and a lot of instruction, they may come to see the light, fully comprehend, and find their way back home.

These last few days have been very painful for me. I've neglected to ask for your help, thereby becoming sad and downhearted. I feel as though you have forsaken me. I've tried very hard to get the lost ones back but nothing seems to work. My heart is breaking because I love them so. Further, some have become arrogant and hateful as they feel betrayed by previous instructions. They are very stubborn and entrenched in their position. Words do not console them. Forgive them, for they know not what they are doing. I think you will have to intercede on their behalf. Give them something of your robust spirit to instill a deep desire for joining us again.

So Father, I ask to come home. I need to hear your calming voice and the roar of your laughter. I long for your gentle embrace and your hugs of encouragement. I thirst for that feeling to be truly alive again. I need to see that sparkle in your eye, your comforting glance, and feel the warmth of your gaze upon me to rekindle the fire in my heart. Then, we'll dance together in the palace of luminous light to joyous music and the exuberant rhythm of life.

Until we meet again, I place my very being in your hands.

Your Loving and Adoring Son,

Jesus the Nazorean

Initially published in the Monterey Observer Newspaper

"It is in dying that we are born to eternal life."

~ *St. Francis of Assisi; Lover of all Creation, Christian Mystic*

THE CRYSTAL

Debra Davis Hinkle, 2008

Twenty-five years
Hanging from the chandelier
A long and lone crystal

Five years
Put away in a drawer
A long and lone crystal

Yesterday, finally
Washed and held the crystal
United it with the sun
A long and lone crystal

Under the prism's shape
Making rainbow's spectrum
Memories of meals past
Floating around the room

Take me back to another time
When his mom was still with us
Before frailty clutched her
Then finally shattered her

Hanging from a new chandelier
A long and lone crystal

GONE BEFORE

Jim Leonard, 2008

Dear Father in Heaven:

Help me say the prayer you gave me.

For my mother and father,
For my family and friends,
For my generation, and
For all who have gone before me.

Raise them into the light of your presence.
Let them be happy serving and praising you.
May you be delighted with their childlike
   curiosity and awe,
As you walk with them in your beautiful garden.

Rescue all that have turned away from you.
Send your mighty angels to battle for their souls.
Move them to a place so all of your children
   can pray for them.
Let these prayers help bring them safely
   home to you.

Amen.

Then say the Our Father, Hail Mary, and
the Jesus Prayer.

"... All life has its rhythms, and the repetition
of familiar prayers can bring our interior
spirits into harmony with the Divine
Heartbeat ..."

~ *Stephen J. Binz; American Scripture Scholar,
Writer, Lecturer*

The Man and the Sapphire

Debra Davis Hinkle, 2008

She gave me two gifts:

One is made of mostly
   oxygen, carbon and hydrogen
His sapphire eyes sparkle like hers
His character formed by her
   dedication, love and teachings
He will live a finite time
But is priceless

The other is corundum
The color comes from
   titanium and iron
Cornflower blue and surrounded
   by diamonds
It will be forever
And grow more expensive

She gave me the greatest gift possible
And, her precious sapphire

I'D RATHER...

Debra Davis Hinkle, 2008

Death and grief, unknown
Before the loss of my mother
Now, they're both known
Only too well

Couldn't leave it at just
Death and grief
Fear made it a trio
Nightmares previewing
Husband's death

Feel death and grief again
Fear, I'd rather die

"The way to love anything is to realize it might be lost."

~ *G.K. Chesterson; English Writer*

1-800-HEAVEN*, SECOND CALL

Debra Davis Hinkle, 2008

Come on telephone—connect and ring. Oh please God, don't let there only be one call to her. Ringing—the greatest sound.

"Hello."

"Mom, I was so afraid—"

"—You wouldn't get to talk to me again."

"Yes, but how …?"

"Honey, I know more things up here."

"I hope you don't know everything!"

"Only God does!"

"Mom, I forgot to tell you …"

"What is it, honey?"

"I got published. I'm an author."

"Congratulations and keep writing because you will be published again."

"How do you know that?"

"The same way I know you are late and we better end

this call!"

"Oh, you're right! I've got to go."

"I love you, honey. Call again, soon."

Click!

"If tears could build a stairway and memories a lane, I'd walk right up to heaven and bring you home again."

~ *Anonymous*

GETTING VELMA TO LAUGH

Jim Leonard, 2007

One of my dearest friends (Velma, age 75) had a series of minor strokes that required hospitalization and extended care. Her youngest daughter (Julie) stepped up to the plate to give Velma all the assistance she could. My letter to Julie in May of 2001 follows.

Dear Julie:

Thanks for the pictures. Velma looks good, not much difference from 1988 (my visit to Spokane) or 1995 (her visit to Anaheim). I am sure that being back in familiar surroundings at home is a great comfort to her, especially to be near her little dog "Nick."

If you get a chance let her know I still enjoy telling the stories about the trip to Spokane, breakfast in the park near her house, all the children running and playing near the lake, later one of them falling in the birdbath in the arboretum. Also, if you jog her memory about the Tonganoxie and Reno Kansas days, she may recall Myrt and Jim's gas station, café, and cabins out on the old highway. That was a time when I helped your oldest sister to walk all by herself.

Let me tell you a story, one that will certainly be in Velma's memory, and she might enjoy hearing it.

> Once upon a time there was a little schoolhouse on the prairie near a small town called Tonganoxie, named after a Cherokee Indian chief. The young woman who taught school there loved all the children and she helped them with their lessons. One afternoon little Jimmie was bouncing all over the place and she couldn't keep him focused on the lesson so she clapped her hands together real hard making a loud noise and said to Jimmie, "Hey, why don't you sit over there and read this book while I teach the class today's lesson?"

> After a few years Jimmie graduated from high school, bought a small grocery store from the Boy Scout Leader, and his business was doing very

well. One afternoon an old woman came into the store and said she wanted to see the owner. The clerk said, "Go into the office back there and the owner will help you." So she went into the office and Jimmie said, "Sit over there Ma'am and I'll be right with you." In a few moments he went over to the old woman and asked, "How can I help you?" The old woman looked directly into his eyes and firmly stated, "I'm looking for that little bastard that wouldn't sit still in my third grade class!" Jimmie's head popped back, his eyes got real big, as he tried to focus on the woman's face. After a few seconds he realized it was indeed his third grade school teacher. With a big smile on his face he greeted her and gave her a big hug. They both laughed for a long time about him not recognizing her.

Now telling this story to my mother a few months back got a big belly laugh out of her and later she said, "Boy, she got him real good!" Velma may remember Wanda the schoolteacher, Bill the Boy Scout Leader, and Jimmie the little squirt in the story. I hope Velma gets a few belly laughs also. Continue to laugh with her and let her know that I love her very much.

* * *

In November of 2001, about a year after my mother passed away, Velma's doctors told Julie that the end was near. Julie brought her mother home again and two days later Velma passed away peacefully in her own bed with her family by her side. The bond between Julie and her mother was so strong that Julie took every opportunity to enjoy her mother's playfulness and teasing even in very difficult situations. I watched this drama from afar, sometimes through tears of sorrow, and at other times through tears of joy while trying to visualize Velma's little antics. I learned two important facts. First, Julie is the champion mentor for showing me the way to help my loved ones pass on to the next life. And second, laughter is good, very good, even when it hurts. I know in my heart that Velma is certainly laughing now and enjoying her new life in heaven.

"Laughter is the best medicine."

~ *Anonymous*

ONE YEAR LATER

Debra Davis Hinkle, 2011

After a horrendous life of being
tormented nightly by
terrifying dreams,
running from evil,
panting in exhaustion,
clawing at my throat
to avoid suffocation,
screaming awake to find
red lines on my neck
like welts from your belt;
then barring the bedroom door—
my nightmares are over.

You are
Dead! Dead! Dead!
And, I'm free.
What took so long?

No guilt here.
It is where it should be—
all yours.

Finally fatherless—
My inner child is
a happy dreamer.

"I've never wished a man dead, but I've read some obituaries with great pleasure."

~ *Mark Twain (pseudonym), Samuel Langhorne Clemens was an American author and humorist.*

REMEMBERING BUFF MOMMA'S TOE FETISH

Debra Davis Hinkle, 2012

She was a lovely cream-colored tabby with light orange stripes. If she was running you'd miss the stripes, they were that faint. Her fur felt like fine silk. She had round mint green eyes that sparkled when she looked at me.

She was Buff Boy's mother. Little Buff Momma had a proclivity for human toes, not feet; and not just anyone's toes—mine to be exact. She loved my appendages, not my heels or my arches—just my toes. Polished or natural, she had to have my digits.

Twice a day I would sit on the wood steps leading from my deck to my backyard and in Buff Momma's own time she came over and sat at my toes, not my feet. Then she would start to smell my toes and rub them with one side of her face and then the other side. This lead to her opening her mouth and a canine hitting my hallux—then drooling and before I knew it she was nibbling on all my phalanges. It seemed like my stinky appendages were catnip infused.

This was a daily ritual for her and for me it was cherished time, one that animal lovers would understand.

"No Heaven would Heaven ever be were it not for my cats there to welcome me."

~*Anonymous*

PHOTO - THE RUBBING BY
BUFF MOMMA

Starting her routine with Debra.

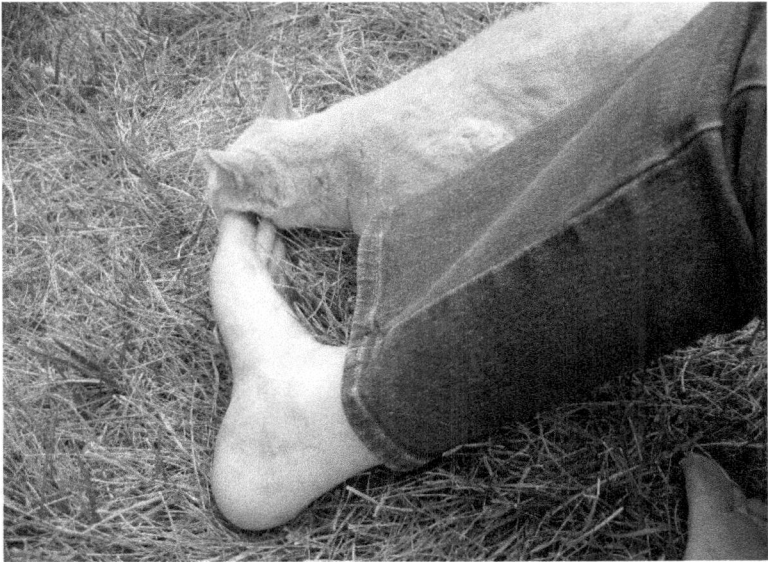

Photo by Debra Davis Hinkle

PHOTO - THE CANINE BY BUFF MOMMA

Continuing her routine with Debra.

Photo by Debra Davis Hinkle

PHOTO - THE NIBBLING BY BUFF MOMMA

Concluding her routine with Debra.

Photo by Debra Davis Hinkle

Buff Momma was one of the adult feral cats that I found in the summer of 2007. She was the first wild cat to let me pick her up. She joined her son, Buff Boy, in Heaven on August 1, 2009. Of all my feral cats that are gone, I miss her the most—her gentleness and toe fetish routine that calmed me down and made me smile.

JOURNAL ENTRY:
WEDNESDAY, SEPTEMBER 14, 2002

Debra Davis Hinkle, 2002

Mom, I wonder if your love and teachings will help heal the grieving daughter who cracked and crumbled upon your death?

Excerpt from: Grieving Daughter, Dying Mother

"Bereavement unravels like a piece of cloth, the fabric of your life. Over time you will be able to reweave your piece of cloth, but the cloth will have a new pattern."

~ Anonymous

UNITING US ONCE MORE

TO MORRIS

Jim Leonard, 2009

Your quiet smile with arms on my shoulders.
How much I love you, you will never know.
I watch you sleeping at my knee
And I yearn to speak with you.

Rousing, you make stretching moves,
Then your nose penetrates my beard.
I know you are happy, signaled by a wagging tail,
Come to me for a good old barrel hug.

I ponder your moods at various times.
They all melt into shining eyes and happy jumps.
Surely you can sense my love,
As I come to your every call.

Often when I wake, you are sleeping on my chest.
Talk to me with your best purrs.
Tell the world you've found what really matters.
Look into my eyes and see the love reflected there.

PHOTO – MORRIS

The Co-Author's Orange Shorthair Tabby in
September 2009.

Photo by Jim Leonard

CONVERSATION WITH MY HUSBAND: 2011

Debra Davis Hinkle, 2011

"It's been too long since I've visited my mother's grave," I told my husband.

"How can you tell?"

"I couldn't find it, even with the cemetery map."

"Grief changes shape, but it never ends."

~ *Keanu Reeves, Canadian Actor*

MY MOTHER

Debra Davis Hinkle, 2009

Be patient toward all that is unsolved in your heart.
   Why did she die at seventy-five?
   How old will I be when I die?
   Will I see her again?
   Does she know how much I loved her?
   Does she know how much I miss her? I hope not.
   Does she miss me? I hope not, too.
   Does the bond die when she does?
   I know it doesn't!
Try to love the questions themselves.

With thanks to Rainer Maria Rilke
"Letters to a Young Poet"
Lines one and ten

"What we have once enjoyed deeply we can never lose. All that we love deeply becomes a part of us."

~ *Helen Keller; American Author, Political Activist, Lecturer*

MY MOTHER, MY MIRROR

Debra Davis Hinkle, 2008

Look in the mirror
What do I see?
See her sometimes
Me others

Look in the mirror
What do I see?
Only me
Where is she?

Lost in the mirror
Looking for one of us
She's dead
And, I'm ...

*   *   *

Look in the mirror
What do I see?
She's alive inside of me
I'm finally okay

Look in the mirror
What do I see?
Someone we are both proud of

SURPRISE ENDING

Jim Leonard, 2009

Just enough room for us in a '37 Chevy to follow
the Oregon Trail to the mighty, mighty Pacific.
Dad's tools, three fuel pumps, and a few tires, just in
case.
Sandwiches, fruit, drinks and we're ready to go.

In Yellowstone we found a few brown bears.
Waving sandwiches out the back windows
brought the bears running toward the car.
Mom got a few pictures before Dad sped away.

Yakima, the gateway to a big snow cone named
Rainier.
July 1947 brought shirtsleeve weather at 7,000 feet.
Dad tricked us and washed our faces in the snow.
Screaming and yelling was not much help.

On to the Oregon coast for a glimpse of the Pacific.
My brother and I played on the beach.
Knocked over in the ocean… surely we would die.
Swallowing saltwater was a scary thing to do.

Snow on Rabbit Ears Pass blocked the way home.
Finding a spare room was quite an ordeal.

Mattress piled on top kept us from freezing.
Three weeks later we're safely back home in Kansas
City.

I didn't know, until years later, that his
passion had become my compulsion.
Without a word, only a smile or two, his
love of nature now delights my soul.

A landscape or seascape warms my heart.
It seems like I'm looking through Dad's eyes.
That's a feeling for me to recall.
That's a feeling best of all.

"... Be praised my Lord for Mother Earth:
abundant source, all life sustaining; she feeds
us bread and fruit and gives us flowers."

~ St Francis of Assisi; Canticle of Creation, 6th
Stanza

THE TRAIN TRIP

Debra Davis Hinkle, 2008

The train rocks, rolls and rumbles
The familiar movements' hum is soothing
But, I have never taken this exact trip before

    I have taken this trip many times
    To visit my mother
    We shop and care for my young nephews

    Many times I have taken this trip
    Escorting my nephews to my home
    Another visit and more memories

    This trip I have taken many times
    To care for my ailing mother
    I am exhausted

    I hoped never to take this trip
    My mother is dead
    I am numb with grief

    I have taken this trip many times
    To visit my sister
    I miss my mother less when I am with my sister

I will never take this trip again
My nephews are too old to visit
And, my sister is moving away

Many times I have taken this trip
To see my uncle Bob
He is all that is left, for me,
In my hometown

The train rocks, rolls and rumbles
The familiar movements' hum is soothing
A new journey unfolds

"The woods are lovely, dark and deep. But I have miles to go before I sleep."

~ *Robert Frost; American Poet*

MOTHERS REMEMBERED

Debra Davis Hinkle, 2009

You're never completely independent
  of your mother
Not even after her death
Love and grief last your lifetime

You see her in your dreams
And remember her warm and loving touch
You hear the fairy tales she softly read
And the nursery rhymes she sang
You smell the food she cooked
And the perfume she wore

If you are very lucky
You feel her love and encouragement

"There are times the memories are not enough.
Will the pain ever ease? Will I ever be able to
accept [that] you are gone forever?"

~ *Anonymous*

PHOTO – MOM

The photo was taken in the kitchen of Debra's childhood home.

Photo from Debra Davis Hinkle's personal family collection

This picture evokes dormant memories of Gingham curtains my mother made and her love of flowers—culinary and baking skills enjoyed while surrounded by family—coupons clipped and waiting for Friday's grocery shopping trip and so much more.

LOSS AND GAIN

Debra Davis Hinkle, 2009

Most that I held dear and
All that I knew was gone
What was left?
I did not know

Death of my mother
Removed the matriarchal glue
Fractured family
Loss of rituals, observances, customs

* * *

It took years to find myself
Started with some great advice—
"Build a new family"

* * *

I was free to choose
Anything and everything
But mostly who I was

How I saw myself
Finally not give a damn
How someone else saw me

They never knew me
They never will know me
Whether I like it or not

*   *   *

I gained myself

"The 'gift' of grief is that it presents us with the opportunity to heal and grow."

~ *Jewish Proverb*

JUST SAY IT

Debra Davis Hinkle, 2008

Should I say it?
No, I'll feel embarrassed
I don't want to be humiliated

I'm too old to say it
You're never too old to speak those words
Just say it

Why do I want to say it?
I want her to hear it
She has already heard it

Maybe, I just want her to hear it, again
Why?
Because!

Even if I'm embarrassed or humiliated
Regardless, of why I want to say it
"Mom, I love you!"

THE BIND

Debra Davis Hinkle, 2010

If there was a second wheelbarrow,
absolutely everything
would not depend upon the red one.

Do I let the animals drink from the wheelbarrow?
Or do I dump the water and fill the
red wheelbarrow with horse poop?

I cannot dump the water
fill the wheelbarrow with poop
then empty the wheelbarrow and
refill it with rainwater for the animals.

It all depends on which is more important—
rainwater or poop.

I'm ankle deep in rainwater and
calf deep in shit.
So poop evacuation it is!

I miss you Finn McCool and
would be happy to give you rainwater and
keep your pasture clean of poop.

If you were still alive
Finn McCool
absolutely everything
would not seem so chickenshit.

Inspiration: William Carlos Williams,
The Red Wheelbarrow

"The way to Heaven is on horseback."

~ *Anonymous*

1-800-HEAVEN*, THIRD CALL

Debra Davis Hinkle, 2009

With the sound of this "ring" I feel fear and hope banded together—fear that I won't hear your voice again and hope that we are eternally connected.

"Hello."

"Mom, you sound different."

"I am different and you sound like you're scared."

"I was afraid—"

"I'm always with you, as is he."

"Sometimes, I'm not sure or I forget."

"It's only human."

"Mom, do you talk to my sisters, too?"

"Yes, just not exactly like I communicate with you."

"I understand."

"Honey, you won't be calling as often in the future."

"I won't?"

"No, you'll be busy and so will I."

"But, —"

"We will be here, whenever you need us.   Bye, honey."

"I love …"

Click!

"Ten years, she's dead, and I still find myself some mornings reaching for the phone to call her. She could no more be gone than gravity or the moon."

~ *Mary Karr; American Poet, Essayist, Author*

STEP INTO THE MIRROR

Jim Leonard, 2008

At present:
   I see imperfectly.
Sometimes:
   I see a hint of things to come.
Meditating:
   I see with the eyes of my heart.
Then:
   I see creation as the Other sees it.
Perfect vision:
   Is in the eye of the Other.

The Other's message:
   Is about love.
With patience, perseverance, and trust:
   I enter the Other's dwelling place and
      The Other's tender loving gaze embraces me.
My love for the Other:
   Requires acceptance of His message.

The Other's design appears:
   As I muse on my reflected image.
   The desire for unity overwhelms my emotions.
   My thoughts always return to the Other.
The Other whispers:

"Think of creation and your image will glow."
My image beckons but is it me or the Other?

Loving the Other is difficult at times.
Seeing the Other in myself softens my heart.
Compassion turns to joy
  as I glimpse the eternal.
I'll gaze on the Other:
  until there is no other.

"I look forward to death with great anticipation, to meeting God face to face."

~ Billy Graham, Preacher, Evangelist

OUR BRIEF VISIT

Debra Davis Hinkle, 2011

If my mom could visit,
I would have a chance to
ask her some questions.

* * *

Did it hurt to pass away?
I thought I would die
without you.
Do you miss me?

At your funeral,
did you notice your
10-year old grandson
held my hand
when I started to cry?
He never let go until
the service was over.
I wrote a poem about
his caring.

Did you see me
win my first writing award?
Do you know

my stories and poems
are published and I just
completed my first book?

Do you know
all your children and
grandchildren
did not speak to each
other for years?
I hope not.

Did you see me this
summer having lunch
with my sister and niece?
The ones I had not
spoken to in over eight years.
I hope so.

Tell me, is God like a
friend, lover, parent—
or all of those?

What is Heaven like?
Do you have a job?
Any cats there?

Are your aunt, parents,
brothers there?
Dad died last year.
I am not sure that
he is in Hell, but
I sure sleep better now.

Do you know when
I will join you?
I will join you, right?
Remember you promised
to make a home there for me.

                    *   *   *

At this point, I'm sure
Mom would run
back to Heaven
to rest her ears.

Maybe I should have
asked if it is
quiet in Heaven?

"Those things that hurt instruct."

~ *Benjamin Franklin; American Author, Politician,
Scientist, Inventor, Musician*

CREED FOR THE THIRD MILLENNIUM

Jim Leonard, 2010

I believe in God, the Father Almighty, creator of the evolutionary universe. I believe in Jesus Christ, his only son, born of the Virgin Mary, was crucified, died, and was buried. On the third day, he arose as the Risen Christ, ascended to the Father, and became the Cosmic Christ, the center of the universe. I believe in the Holy Spirit, the breath of life, who transforms the human heart into hearts of love of God and love of neighbor. I believe in the power of contemplation, with the help of the Holy Spirit, we radiate spiritual energy, and assist the Cosmos to move into the future.

Origin of the prayer: Last night, 10/04/2010, was our class graduation at the Monastery of the Risen Christ. For the event all of the students were asked to provide their conclusions on

Ilia Delio's book, *Christ in Evolution*. The conclusions were celebrated during the liturgy of the Word, as part of Father Steve Coffey's Homily. My contribution was an updated Creed, a statement of belief (faith) for use by Christian Catholics.

"Even though I walk through the darkest valley, I fear no evil; for you are with me; your rod and your staff—they comfort me."

~ *Psalm 23:4; NRSV*

MEETING ROLAND'S MOTHER

Debra Davis Hinkle, 2007

Roland said, "It's only a week-end at my parents' house; it will be so easy."

I'd like to say I was poised when meeting my boyfriend's parents for the first time. But, I was a nervous wreck after I got the tour of his childhood home. I'd never been in such a nice home—hardwood floors, oriental carpets and antique furniture in every room. Roland saw my "deer in the headlights" look and came to my rescue.

"Honey, everything is going to be fine. Just relax."

"You didn't tell me your parents were rich."

"They aren't."

"What do you call all these antiques?"

"Old junk. ... Why don't you ask Mom if she needs any help?"

"I can do that, my mom taught me how to help in the kitchen."

"Great."

* * *

"May I help you with dinner?"

"Yes, would you set the table?"

"I would be happy to." Oh, boy the easy job, and then I look at the dining room table! Linen tablecloth and napkins. What are these small forks and little round spoons? Who eats with all these forks? Big ones, long ones, short ones and curved ones. Real silver, too, I think.

And, that was just the beginning!

I look around at the crystal glasses and I know I'm in deep shit! Do I set the glass to the right or the left and is this a water glass or a wine goblet? If only I hadn't ditched all those home economic classes in high school.

Where is my boyfriend when I need him? He's probably sitting in his favorite "antique" chair.

I'm humming a Dance of the Fairy Forks, waiting for the stupid forks to rise up, do the dance and then sit down at their assigned places.

No dancing silver tonight. I can't get out of this so I tiptoe into the kitchen and whisper, "What are the small forks and little round spoons for and where do I put them?"

She smiles at me, "You know I'm not sure, but I think the small forks are for ..."

Years later, I knew she was being kind for my sake. Now every time I touch her linen, silver or crystal I remember her smile and kind words.

"Grief shared is grief diminished."

~ *Rabbi Grollman; American Author, Counselor*

MELROSE LOVED DEBBY

Debra Davis Hinkle, 2009

The sweetest rose in the entire garden, how did I ever get so lucky to have you as my mom?

I inscribed those words to my mother-in-law, Melrose, in a copy of my first publication, *Tales From The Corner, an Anthology* that was released in December 2005. The inscription and my signature on the cover page was a heartfelt dedication to her for the unconditional love she showed me from the instant of our very first meeting.

I was happy and proud to place the book in her hands. She closed her arthritic hands around it and gave me a loving and welcoming smile. Her love was also reflected from her beautiful big blue eyes.

Five months later she was gone, the day before my birthday. Mom was ninety-two. Some people would say she lived a long and full life, but what do they know?

In a cruel twist of fate, or maybe a stroke of irony, I

celebrated my birthday packing up Mom's room at the care facility. There I was sorting through her clothes—feeling sad, but determined. When my heart was too heavy to continue, I took a break and thought I would share the book's dedication with Mom's Filipino caregiver, Malaya.

However, it was Malaya who shared a poignant story with me. Her unforgettable story began with "Melrose loved Debby." She said that while walking across the room. Then she held up the book I had given Mom. She told me that Mom slept with my book on her chest every night.

Malaya had no idea that I was Debby, the person who had written a short story and skit that was proudly printed on pages 139 and 209 and also wrote the dedication to her. Malaya was just sharing a heartfelt memory of Melrose.

I was trying to put everything together, the memory and the realization of what I had meant to my mother-in-law, but it was too much, too soon. My wound was too fresh and too deep. It was then I heard, her voice, distinct and clear in my head. "Happy Birthday, Dear," her pet name for me.

Thanks, Mom for the best present ever—your love!

Thanks to Anne Schroeder for her invaluable critique.

"With the gift of listening comes the gift of healing."

~ *Catherine Doherty; Foundress of Madonna House.*

THE KNITTING CHAIR

Debra Davis Hinkle, 2009

When I was a child my mother, with infinite patience, taught me how to knit. She settled into her recliner and I sat on its arm, observing first and later knitting. I never got further than just one light pink bootie. My lack of perseverance disappointed both of us.

The first Christmas after my mother's death, I splurged on a book—*Stitch and Bitch: The Knitter's Handbook* by Debbie Stoller, whose title appealed to the whiner in me. The book would be a stand-in for my mother's no longer available lessons.

Late one evening I sat in my mother's old chair with the book open, pink yarn wrapped around one hand and a knitting needle in my other.

I decided to make a scarf and I tried to cast on stitches. I read the how-to section three times, but I couldn't figure out how to cast on the first stitch. The illustrations didn't help, either.

What little patience I had was gone. First frustration and then anger set in and I began to cry. I don't know how long I cried, but without thinking about it, I had cast on the stitches from memory. Perhaps my mother was sitting on the arm of her recliner giving me a refresher course. Regardless, I wiped away my tears and proceeded to knit the most beautiful light pink scarf.

*   *   *

In the nine years following my mother's death, I've knitted scarves, hats and many pairs of socks all with her help from above. We've changed places, though. I'm comfy in her chair and her spirit hovers nearby.

*   *   *

My mother's chair is extremely worn and I would like to have it reupholstered in a leopard print. Some people would say, "Your mother will roll over in her grave if you do that to her chair."

To them I say, "It's time for her to roll over, she's probably getting sore in one position anyway."

My mother taught me to knit and she gave me her love of cats. We will be knitting together in our newly leopard upholstered chair until I join her in heaven. Knit, purl. Knit, purl. Knit, purrrrr.

"Joy comes, grief goes, we know not how."

~ *James Russell Lowell; American Poet, Critic, Editor, Diplomat*

TAKE AWAY

Debra Davis Hinkle, 2009

Take away my fears
Take away my tears
Take away the abuse
Let me loose

Take away the loss
Take away the pain
Take away the grief
Let me loose

* * *

Take away my memories
You take away my life

> "Given a choice between grief and nothing, I'd choose grief."
>
> ~ *William Faulkner; American Writer, Nobel Prize Laureate*

A GREAT TEACHER

Debra Davis Hinkle, 2010

Taught me to trust myself, simply
  by trusting me enough to
    roll in the sand at my feet,
      on our second day together.

    Schooled me to post a jackhammer trot
    by patiently teaching me over a long time,
  first with the sissy strap attached to the saddle and
me holding on for dear life.

Inspired me to canter
  by the grace of God,
    his experience with multiple riders and
      much fear on my part.

    Steeled me to jump
    by doing all the work for me,
  letting me just lean forward and
pray I wouldn't end up breaking my neck.

Filled my heart to overflowing
  by returning my love and
    showing his many skills and quirks
      while training me.

Slammed me to my knees
forty-eight days ago,
my handsome boy,
Finn McCool unexpectedly died.

* * *

My unforgettable teacher and
beloved horse gave me
great memories, riding skills and
much needed self-confidence.

"There is something about the outside of a
horse that is good for the inside of a man
[woman]."

~ *Winston Churchill; English Prime Minister*

PHOTO – FINN McCOOL

Debra's Chestnut Colored Irish Warmblood Horse at
Montaña de Oro in June 2008.

Photo by Lynaia Fallscheer

Finn McCool died in June 2010.

OPENING MY HEART

Debra Davis Hinkle, 2011

Finn McCool—
Seventeen hands
Fourteen hundred pounds
Gigantic and heavy feet
Difficult to pick hoof
Good at dressage
Great jumper
Calm temperament
Ticklish sides
Magnificent
Irish Warmblood

Only seventeen and
Taken from me last June
I hit the linoleum at
His passing
Heart broken
Grieved this past year
For my beloved Chestnut

This June, Sundance
Entered my life

Just sixteen hands
Only twelve hundred pounds
With normal size feet—
Might be able to hold
His foot up and pick it
No dressage training
Can he jump?
Seems relaxed
Ticklish?
Quarter horse

Fourteen
But he could still die
Anytime

Heart now open
Found room enough
For me to love another—
A Palomino

"Sometimes the hardest part isn't letting go,
it's starting over."

~ *Nicole Sobon; American Writer*

PHOTO – SUNDANCE

Debra's husband riding their new Palomino in 2011.

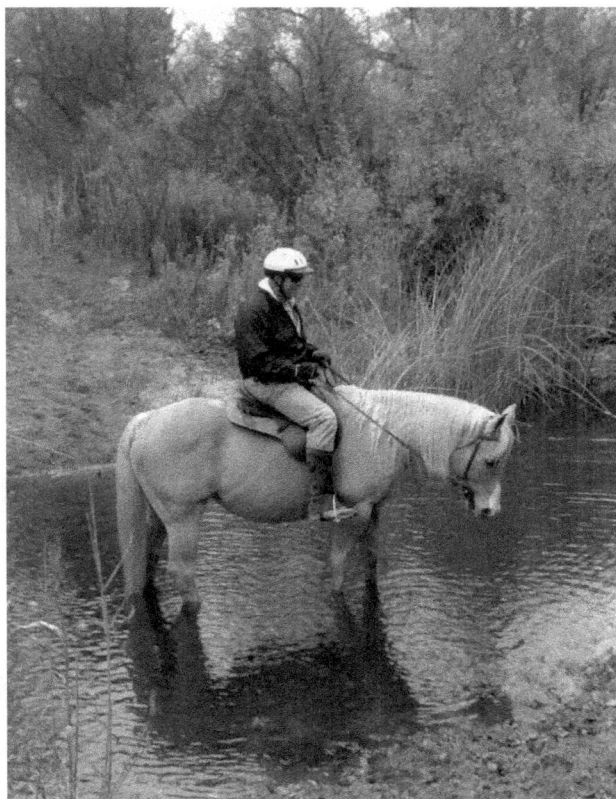

Photo by Lynaia Fallscheer

Whether it was grief, or because I was no longer riding, I didn't develop a loving and lasting relationship with Sundance. With great regret and to give Sundance a better home, he was sold in July 2012.

MY BEST FRIEND AND TEACHER

Debra Davis Hinkle, 2007

Some things were easy to instruct
Beading and needlepoint
Sewing and knitting
Baking, not cooking

Other things were best shown, not taught
The difference between right and wrong
Never swearing
I got right and wrong, but damn I missed swearing

Along the way, my teacher instilled in me
Honesty, empathy and kindness
A great love of all animals—
Especially cats

Some of her favorite words to me:
"Look before you leap."
"Just because so and so does it …"
"I know you'll always tell me the truth."

My teacher showed me how to garden and arrange
  flowers
To appreciate and collect Depression glass
She trained me in art of Christmas shopping
Before and after

She tutored me about God and heaven
Faith I had to learn the hard way
After she was gone

She was a great friend and teacher
Her frequent lesson—
Patience
Finally learned during her last illness—
Cancer—
Took her just six years ago

I miss you, Mom
But, you're still teaching me

"You gain strength, courage, and confidence
by every experience in which you really stop
to look fear in the face. You must do the thing
which you think you cannot do."

~ *Eleanor Roosevelt, American First Lady,
Diplomat, Author*

PHOTO – MOM AND ME

Debra and her mother on a camping trip in 1958.

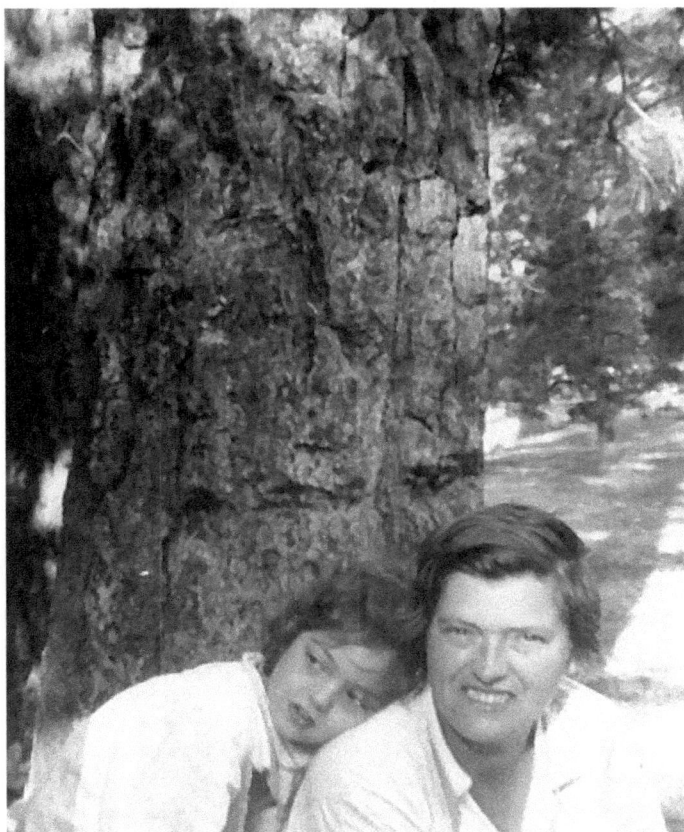

Photo from Debra Davis Hinkle's Family Photo collection

THE LAST PLACE

Debra Davis Hinkle, 2010

Frightened child
Needed you near
Terrified without you
Searching for you

Now you are gone
No longer on earth
Journey ended

Grieving adult
Searching
For you
For me, too
Journey begins

* * *

Can talk to you—but are you listening?
Can see you—only in my dreams
Can hear you—in my mind
Can remember you—easily and always
Afraid to forget
Afraid I will forget

Looked everywhere for you
I finally found you
In the last place

Looked inside of me
Right where you were—all the time
No longer afraid
Learning to trust myself

"Death leaves a heartache no one can heal, love
leaves a memory no one can steal."

~ *From a headstone in Ireland*

Together, Again

Debra Davis Hinkle, 2011

Heaven
Waits
For
You,
No
More

Someday
Heaven's
Gates
Will
Welcome
Me

Uniting
Us
Once
More

Excerpt from the poem Buff Boy with modifications to the second stanza. Stanzas were used as chapter headings.

OTHER CONTRIBUTORS' WORK

CHRISTINE'S MOTHER

Anne Schroeder

"Christine's mother walks her to the bus stop," Katy remarked, twisting her toast into bite-size pieces then setting them back on the plate. "Christine's lucky."

Reaching to clear a handful of breakfast dishes from the table, I brushed a kiss across Katy's forehead and cheerfully agreed. "I guess Christine's mother loves her better."

Katy glanced up, surprised. "No she doesn't ..." she started to protest, then grinned when she realized I was kidding her. I sent her off with a hug, cautioning her to hurry or she'd miss her early-bird bus. With a twinge of guilt I watched my second-grader, bundled in her bright-blue goose down jacket and red stocking cap, running down the long driveway in the gray, frosty morning. But she skipped ahead to catch up with a friend and I started my daily routine.

That evening while I tucked her into bed, Katy reached to twist a strand of my hair and quietly told me, "Christine's mother took her to McDonald's for lunch and bought her a lip gloss and she came back to school just before recess ended. Can we do that tomorrow?"

I smiled and replied, "You bet ... sometime. But not tomorrow. Daddy's taking the car and we sure can't walk that far. But sometime soon ... promise."

As I left the room and gently closed the door, I thought, Christine is a most indulged little girl. Christine, who skated backward on her own set of rink skates, who came out with the first computer game system in the neighborhood, whose mother walked her to the bus stop and who is leading my daughter into unrealistic expectations of life.

I decided that if Katy felt so strongly about the attention Christine was getting, I would break out of my comfortable routine and do something about it. The next morning I dressed early and surprised her by suggesting that I walk her to the bus stop. We packed cinnamon toast and orange juice and had a picnic on a little knoll where we fed our crusts to a kitten that came by to investigate. We began a sometimes ritual of walking together and I came to know the Froggy Pond, The Path, the friendly dog and the children at the bus stop.

One day I met Christine's mother. After waving our children off through the back window of the disappearing yellow bus, we strolled the short distance home. Pausing at the end of my driveway, I asked her up for a cup of tea. To my surprise she accepted, and for the next two hours we shared confidences. She told me about her oldest son's musical ability, her hopes that one of her children would become a doctor and how hard it was to join a busy family together for family dinner and prayer. Gradually, hesitantly, Donna told me of her leukemia and her numerous trips to the hospital for chemotherapy, her intolerance to germs and her fears that Christine would not have the time with her that the older children had enjoyed.

After she left I sat a long time just looking out my window. Finally I reached for the phone and deliberately dialed the number. The voice on the other end said, "Hello ... Santa Rosa Elementary. Mrs. Anderson

178 TEARS TO LAUGHTER

speaking."

"Yes, hello ... This is Mrs. Schroeder. Could I leave a message for Katy in Room 5? I will be picking her up for lunch today ... but I'll have her back by the end of lunch recess."

Seven months have passed and Donna is still bravely battling her illness. Christine and Katy are best friends, second-grade style. Every day when the sun comes up over our neighborhood, I say a prayer for the lady who helped me to see my world through new eyes. A very special lady—Christine's mother.

(Christine's mother, Donna Braun, died three months after I wrote these words. Before her death I gave her a copy. At her request, the minister included it in her eulogy. In the years that have passed, Donna's daughters have grown into lovely, gracious, spirit-filled women. She would be proud of her children. And I believe she would be grateful for the aunts, stepmothers, teachers, neighbors—the women who took the time to help form them.)

Anne Schroeder chronicles her attempts at a balanced life in her humorous, insightful memoir, Ordinary Aphrodite.

SUMMER OF '72

Susan Tuttle

I watched you
through days of unspoken anguish,
   months of silent pain
   unasked questions
crowding your teasing eyes.

And I did not see.

I made you into who I
wanted you to be,
quiet little brother grown,
   so proud of the man
   you'd become,
And watched with giddy glee
   the girls
   drawn
to your lighted soul
   all that summer long.

Or was it the aura of
Little-Boy-Lost
   so subtle I was unaware,
or a darkness hidden deep
beneath layers of devil-may-care,
that moth-fluttered souls

younger than I –
more perceptive than I –
to the fragile flame
of you…

I did not see
though I looked and smiled
  and laughed
    and dreamed…

So unaware.

Where were you that summer,
while your body surfed the waves
  drank the sun
and turned so many heads,
and your smile gladdened hearts
  quickened dreams,
  and your humor lured
the beach-world to your feet?

Where were you
that you could not speak,
  could not reach out,
could not trust or share.
    Could not live.

And now I see, eyes open at last,
heart yearning
  hungering for a future
    foreshortened…

I see now, my eyes wide open

with nothing left to see ...
   too late.

And still I wonder:
Where were you?
   Where are you now?

Susan Tuttle is an editor and Award-winning author of the Write It Right *e-Book series now available on Kindle and author of* Tangled Webs, *a print novel of suspense, available on* www.amazon.com.

WHERE IS HEAVEN?

Helen Sherry, Ph.D.

I miss my Daddy. Miss him, miss him, miss him. Sometimes I just feel sick with the missing. Like a punch in the tummy. Or all the air's been sucked out of me. Everybody says he's in Heaven, but I just don't get where that is. Grandma pointed up, but all I saw were clouds. I'm scared to ask Mama. If I even say the word 'Daddy,' she gulps and shakes her head. Gulping glues the tears behind her eyes. Then her face freezes so a smile couldn't fit.

Like now, tucking me in. Too bad my green eyes remind her of Daddy. Her blue ones are like a butterfly landing everywhere but on mine. Her hand pats down my tangly black hair.

"We should've brushed your hair after your bath, Bethie. Hair like ours is pretty hard to do. Especially when you're seven." She's talking to me, but staring at the patchwork quilt that Grandma made so long ago.

"Didn't know your quilt was torn. Almost like a line of the blue-and-yellow squares are missing. Oh well, I'll patch it. But not tonight and not tomorrow. Night, Sweetie."

The light flicks off and I'm alone upstairs in the dark. No hair brushing, no bedtime stories, no smiles.

I knock the screen off my window checking for Heaven again. Oops! Leaning way, way out, I'm up high, but nothing's different. No angels. Only stars. I miss Daddy … miss his bear hugs…miss counting those stars, 'one bazillion, two bazillion…' and making up silly names for far-away planets. Is Heaven in between Shines-a-lot and Glimmery-Glow-er?

This is an excerpt from her book Where is Heaven?

Helen M. Sherry Ph.D. is a licensed MFCC whose passion is helping people heal from traumas and pain into happier lives. For over 30 years she has loved working with children and teens. Her books help children deal with tough issues. Helen can be reached at www.liveandgrow.com or cqhs2@me.com.

FOREVER THE WAY

Helen Elizabeth Tully Stenger, 1995

One or the other must leave,
One or the other must stay.
One or the other must grieve,
That is forever the way.
That is the vow that was sworn,
Faithful 'til death do us part.
Braving what had to be borne,
Hiding the ache in the heart.
One, howsoever adored,
First must be summoned away.
That is the will of the Lord,
One or the other must stay.

*Helen Elizabeth Tully Stenger passed away in 2005. She was full of life,
loved the Lord (and St. Francis), and she was a gifted writer. Her
Untitled poem was written upon her husband's death in 1995. She is also
the mother of Dr. Mary Kay Stenger, author and reviewer of this book,*
Tears to Laughter.

HELEN'S LAST DAYS OF GLORY

Mary Kay Stenger, 2005

In October of 2005, my 85 year-old mother, Helen Elizabeth Tully Stenger, required in-home hospice care. Despite these challenging circumstances, she retained much of her mental sharpness. She always found the sunny side of everything due to her easy-going nature and playful Irish demeanor. She was completely ready to meet her Maker, but found herself clinging to life inspired by family and friends.

Nighttime was confusing because she was now sleeping most of the day. Two nights in a row she talked about her "travels" at night, specifically to Mexico. Mother always had a great imagination while spinning a tale, so my sister Meg and I were curious about where this might be heading, especially since she actually had not spent much time in Mexico!

One night, Mom started yelling, "Help, help, help

me!" I leaped out of my bed and raced to her side, sending a bedside stand crashing to the floor. She asked, "Do you know how to get out of here?"

"Yes. But we don't need to be going anywhere at 4 o'clock in the morning."

"Where is your mother?"

"YOU are my mother."

"Oh, for heaven's sake!"

Later she asked, "Have you ever been in jail?"

I flippantly answered, "No. Have you?"

With a hint of a conspiracy smile she said, "Yes, and I think you should know about it." Then she began, "I was with friends and it was near my birthday …"

"Mardi Gras?"

"Yes, that is it!"

"Why did you go to jail?"

"I can't remember …"

"What was it like in jail?"

"Oh, it was OK, they brought us meals on a tray!"

"Did you like the food?"

"Oh yes, it was very good!"

I was on the verge of accepting this long-held secret admission about her wild side, when the lopsided reality of things came back into focus: Good food in jail? No way! Then I remembered one of her favorite axioms "Never let the truth get in the way of a good story!"

On one of her last mornings, a minister was bringing Holy Communion. Hearing that a minister was coming she perked up, smiled, and placed her hands over her heart. Following communion, her appearance radiated joy and peace. She looked very much renewed and alive, and this sacred moment seemed to mirror her lifelong faith journey. She said, "The most important thing in life is to stay close to God. He holds you in the palm of His hand." Then holding out her hand, she pointed to her palm.

Her life had prepared her for this moment of transition and she was ready, willing, and excited to meet her God, the Father, whom she came to know from her friend, Jesus. When she closed her eyes for the last time, I am sure that a big party kicked off to welcome her into Heaven! Imagine the laughter and great stories being told now that Helen is on the scene!

Dr. Mary Kay Stenger Ph.D., RN, CHT is a Medical and Clinical Hypnotherapist in the California Central Coast area. She is an author with internationally published research articles in the fields of grief and healing. She is also the mother of six adult children, including three surviving quadruplets.

ACKNOWLEDGEMENTS

Special thanks to the members of the Friday Night Writers' Group for their encouragement and helpful suggestions: Carter Pittman, Destry Ramey, Christine Taylor, Susan Tuttle, and Laurie Woodward.

We are grateful to SLONightWriters for the many writer friends we have met over the years.

By Debra Davis Hinkle and Jim Leonard

AUTHORS' FAVORITE BOOKS ON BEREAVEMENT

Grief and Healing

Davies, Phyllis. *Grief: Climb Toward Understanding: Self-help When You Are Struggling.* Sunnybank Publishers, 1998. Print.

James, John W. and Friedman, Russell. *The Grief Recovery Handbook: The Action Program for Moving Beyond Death, Divorce, and Other Losses.* Harper Collins, 2009. Print.

Prayer and Spiritual

Delio, Ilia, OSF; Warner, Keith Douglass, OFM; Wood, Pamela. *Care for Creation: A Franciscan Spirituality of the Earth.* St. Anthony Messenger Press, 2008. Print.

Huston, Paula, OSB Oblate. *Forgiveness: Following Jesus into Radical Loving.* Paraclete Press, 2008. Print.

Rupp, Joyce, OSM. *Praying our Goodbyes: A Spiritual Companion Through Life's Losses and Sorrows.* Ave Maria Press, 2009. Print.

ABOUT THE AUTHORS

Author **Debra Davis Hinkle** writes memoirs, poems and short stories about grief issues, child abuse, learning disabilities and her passion for animals, especially cats. She is an adult survivor of child abuse and deals with learning disabilities. Debra has six cats and a dog. She is an award winning writer and poet. Some of her work is in *Tales from the Corner, An Anthology*, published by Central Coast Press, which is available at www.amazon.com. She can be reached at debradavishinkle@pacbell.net.

Co-author **Jim Leonard** writes poems, prayers, and short stories about his spiritual journey with the Old Mission Catholic Church in San Luis Obispo, CA. Mr. Leonard is also an Oblate at the Benedictine Monastery of the Risen Christ in San Luis Obispo, CA and his passion involves helping people find their spiritual path. In 2005, Trafford Publishing issued his book *A Little Bible Guide For Carly*. Some of his short stories were published by the Monterey Observer, a Catholic newspaper and also in *Tales from the Corner, An Anthology*, published by Central Coast Press. These books are available at www.amazon.com. He can be reached at jamesleonard08@gmail.com.

If the stories in this book moved you, please visit our
website for more inspiration:

www.kritiquekritics.com/tearstolaughter